03/2013

For my brother Sam,
the sailor

Henry Holt and Company, LLC, *Publishers since 1866*
175 Fifth Avenue
New York, New York 10010
www.HenryHoltKids.com

Henry Holt® is a registered trademark of Henry Holt and Company, LLC.
Text copyright © 2008 by Frances Lincoln Limited
Photographs copyright © 2008 by Oxfam GB and the individual
photographers as named
All rights reserved.
First published in the United States in 2009 by Henry Holt and Company
Originally published in the United Kingdom in 2008 by Frances Lincoln
Children's Books
Distributed in Canada by H. B. Fenn and Company Ltd.

Library of Congress Cataloging-in-Publication Data
Hollyer, Beatrice. / Our world of water : children and water around the world /
Beatrice Hollyer.
p.   cm.
Includes bibliographical references.
ISBN-13: 978-0-8050-8941-7 / ISBN-10: 0-8050-8941-1
1. Water-supply—Juvenile literature. 2. Water—Juvenile literature. I. Title.
TD348.H65 2009   363.6'1—dc22   2008040596

Printed in China on acid-free paper. ∞

10 9 8 7 6 5 4 3 2 1

We would like to thank all the children who took part in *Our World of Water* and their families and communities for their enthusiastic support. We would also like to thank the photographers who spent time with the six children featured in the book:

Amin from the Drik Photo Agency went to Gaibandha in Bangladesh to see Saran and his family.

Annie Bungeroth traveled to Ethiopia to take pictures of Gamachu in his village near the town of Dubluk. Later she flew to Macusani in Peru to spend time with Lucas.

Caroline Irby visited Tajikistan to take photographs of Barfimoh in the village of Pista Mazor, near the border with Afghanistan.

Geoff Sayer spent time with Khadija and her family at their home in Nouakchott, the capital city of Mauritania.

Sungwan So went to see Dahlys in Arcadia, near Los Angeles, California, in the U.S.A.

Oxfam GB will receive a royalty for each copy of this book sold in the United States.
Oxfam is a Registered Charity no. 202918.

Oxfam believes that everyone is entitled to a life of dignity and opportunity and works with poor communities,
partner organizations in different countries, volunteers, and supporters to make this a reality. Oxfam's Education and
Youth Program supports this work by enabling children and young people to understand their world
and to make a positive difference in it. [www.oxfam.org.uk/education]

Our World of Water

Children and Water Around the World

Beatrice Hollyer

Foreword by Zadie Smith

Henry Holt and Company • New York

In association with Oxfam

Our World

Mauritania: Khadija
I live by the sea, where it is very windy. We keep water in a big pottery jar. My favorite drink is sour milk with sugar.

U.S.A.: Dahlys
I live near the Pacific Ocean. I love gardening and watering the vegetables and flowers that grow in our yard. My favorite drinks are water and hot chocolate.

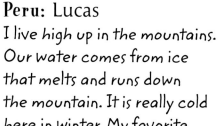

Peru: Lucas
I live high up in the mountains. Our water comes from ice that melts and runs down the mountain. It is really cold here in winter. My favorite drink is homemade lemonade.

# of Water

Bangladesh: Saran
I live in a village surrounded by rivers. In the summer it rains so much that sometimes we have floods. I really like to drink fruit juice.

Tajikistan: Barfimoh
I live among hills and mountains. We collect water every day from a spring at the bottom of a hill. I like to drink water, tea, and milk.

Contents

Ethiopia: Gamachu
I live in very dry countryside where we need to walk a long way to find water for our cattle. My favorite drink is tea.

Foreword

A Book About Water?

This book is about water.

For many people in the developed world, water doesn't seem a very interesting topic. It's everywhere—so obvious and so simple! It flows from our taps into our glasses, into our cooking pots and kettles. It's in our sinks, our baths, our toilets. We don't have to walk very far. We certainly don't have to carry it anywhere. It's in the kitchen, in the bathroom, in a hose in our gardens. Sometimes we even leave it running while we do something else. Some of us have even flushed our toilets to get rid of a single tissue that we couldn't be bothered to put in the trash. When we do things like this we think: *Well, it's only water.* Just turn on the tap and there it is!

We forget what a miracle water is. We forget that it supports everything that lives—humans, animals, plants; the sea, the rivers, the mountains; the atmosphere, the air; when we study other planets in the solar system we know for certain that only those with water could ever have sustained life. Without water, we're nothing at all. Unfortunately, sometimes we take this fact for granted. We have a funny human habit of valuing only what seems rare to us, things like masterpieces of art or diamonds. We think that water is so very common that we needn't value it so highly. But as this book shows, water is not at all as common as we like to think, and we need to value it just as much as paintings and diamonds. Even more, because without it we cannot live.

The True Value of Water

The children in this book use water in lots of different ways. Apart from drinking it, they use it for cooking, washing their food, washing themselves, their clothes, and anything else that needs to be clean; they give it to the animals they look after, because animals need water to live, just as we do. They use water to grow the plants they need to make their food. Children in the developed world also need water for all these reasons, even if they don't do all these tasks themselves. Maybe it is only when you do these tasks yourself that you understand the true value of water.

In developed countries, it is easy to think of a tap as a magical thing, out of which flows an endless supply of clean water—and all you have do is turn it on.

In fact, water systems in developed countries rely on many people behind the scenes who recycle, cleanse, and reuse our water, and so make sure that we always have what seems like more than enough. But we should still look after it: It takes energy, time, and space to cleanse the water. And it is not unlimited. Climate change is causing weather and rainfall patterns to change, which means that many people won't be able to rely on the rain in the way they did before.

A reliable and local supply of fresh water and good sanitation would enhance the lives of millions of people in developing countries. It would protect them from illnesses and enable them to spend less time and energy collecting water.

If you are reading this book and have your own plentiful water supply, maybe the stories will make you think twice about the way you use water. When I finished this book I walked out into the streets of the city I live in—a city that rains plentifully in the wintertime, that is full of fountains, that has a river running straight through it—and I realized that suddenly all the water I could see looked incredibly precious. When I got home I made a list of all the ways I could be less wasteful with the water I use. I think that whenever I am tempted again to think *Well, it's only water,* I will pick up this book and take a lesson from the children you are about to meet, because they know better.

Zadie Smith
Rome, Italy

Peru

Lucas Riquelme lives in Macusani, a small town high up in the mountains of Peru. His family has always farmed alpacas for their wool, but when Lucas grows up, he wants to be a civil engineer. At the moment, Macusani's water comes from melted ice that runs down from the top of the mountains, but climate change is causing the glaciers to shrink and there is less water.

Lucas and his younger brother and sister all love homemade lemonade— water with sugar and fresh lemon juice. Lucas's mother makes it for them at the family's small grocery store in the center of town. She runs the shop while Lucas's father looks after the animals.

"Whenever I drink water, I always put lemon in it."

Winter in the mountains is freezing cold. His house has no heating or hot water, so first thing in the morning, Lucas washes his face and hands very quickly. When it is time for a bath, his mother heats water on the stove.

Sometimes there are cuts in the water supply and the taps don't work. Lucas and his family collect water and keep it in buckets and bowls in the hallway in case this happens.

"Water is important. It is what gives life!"

Lucas needs a big, hot breakfast to keep him warm at school in the icy weather. He eats rice, fried cheese, beef, potatoes, and salad. To drink, he has a cup of thin porridge.

Lucas is proud of his special white baton and the gold braid he wears on his school uniform. They show that he is the class monitor. He is in charge of getting all his classmates to line up for the morning roll call.

At school, Lucas learns about how water is used in farming, and how climate change is making a difference in daily life. The mountain above Macusani used to be white, completely covered with snow and ice. Today, he can see most of the bare mountain.

Lucas lives a short walk from his school, so there is always time for a game of soccer with his friends before and after lessons and during break. He's a big fan of the Brazilian national team.

"We have to wash our hands and faces after playing soccer. The water is freezing cold!"

At break time, the children have cookies and a cup of porridge. Lucas is hungry after playing soccer in the cold wind, so he gets in line for more if there is any left. He has to wash his mug before giving it back.

After school, Lucas does his homework behind the counter at the family grocery store. There's time for another game of soccer before it gets too cold and dark to play outdoors.

A special time for Lucas: A weekend at the ranch

Lucas looks forward to the weekend, when he goes to the family ranch higher up the mountain. His father farms a herd of eight hundred alpacas. Lucas keeps warm in the icy weather in his sweater and traditional Peruvian hat made from natural brown and white alpaca wool.

"This is the alpaca capital of the world!"

Although he has a special pet alpaca named Oscar, Lucas enjoys looking after the whole herd. He helps to give them medicine, check their teeth, and make sure their fleece is free of ticks. The alpacas use highland marshes as their watering holes.

"Oscar always comes running when he sees me. He eats leaves out of my hand."

The farmhouse has no running water or stove. Lucas is in charge of fetching water from a nearby stream. He takes a bucket to collect water every time it's needed, so it is always fresh.

"There's a spring at the top of the hill. My dad put in this pipe to bring the water closer to the house."

Lucas also helps his mother wash clothes. He lights the fire to heat water and helps to fill the plastic tubs with warm water.

"I help to scrub the clothes, then I lay them on rocks to dry in the wind and sun."

Pedro is the family's alpaca herder. When they have finished their chores, he takes Lucas fishing on a nearby lake. They use poles to push their raft into the water, then they look for a good place to drop their net.

"Water is especially important in the countryside. We need it for the alpacas."

Mauritania

Khadija Sow is eight years old. She lives near the Atlantic Ocean
in Mauritania in northwest Africa. Her home is in Nouakchott, the capital city.
It is hot and sandy because the wind blows from the Sahara.
People call the desert "The Snow of Sand."

Khadija lives with her four-year-old sister,
Aîcha, her mother, grandfather,
grandmother, aunts, uncles, and cousins.
Her father is away, working in Tunisia.
Khadija and her sister talk to him every
day on the phone.

It hardly ever rains, so water is precious. Khadija's family stores drinking water in a big pottery jar. It stands in a shady corner of the courtyard inside their house and keeps their water cool in the hot weather. Khadija takes a drink from the jar when she is thirsty. Some people buy their water in metal barrels, but Khadija's house has running water. There is one tap inside the house. All day long, people use this tap to fill buckets, bowls, and kettles, to fill the storage jar, and to wash and cook. Dirty water is carried outside and tipped into a drain close to the house.

"When the weather is hot, I drink a lot of water. Everyone does. We have to keep filling the storage jar."

Brightly colored kettles are used for washing hands at mealtimes and to wash before prayer. The kettles are plastic, so they can't go on the gas stove. Water for tea is heated in metal kettles. The tea is made with fresh mint leaves and lots of sugar, and drinking it is an important part of daily life. But Khadija prefers chocolate milk made with powdered milk and water.

"We don't use lots of water. If I spoil water by making it dirty, my mother will be very cross with me. Other people need it for washing and drinking, so we try not to waste water."

School is just a few minutes' walk away, and Khadija enjoys math and French. When they are thirsty at school, the children dip a cup into a bucket. That way, they don't waste the water from the tap.

"If the water in the bucket looks dirty, then I go to the tap instead."

Khadija comes home for lunch. She eats some fish and rice. In the evening, she waters the two trees outside the house. Her older cousin, Mbolou, feeds and waters the family's animals.

"The sheep drink a lot of water. We give them the water we have used for washing rice. We catch the water that drips from the storage jar and use it to water the trees. We need the trees for shade from the sun."

Khadija's favorite place is the beach outside the town. Her family sometimes goes there for a picnic. Khadija knows how to swim, but she is nervous about the waves, so she just wades today. At the fisherman's beach nearby, Khadija's aunt buys fish that has just been brought in by the wooden fishing boats.

"We swim, and then we eat, and then we swim, and then we eat again. The sea is water, but we can't drink it."

A special time for Khadija: Celebrating Tabaski

Eid al-Adha, or the Festival of Sacrifice, is an important part of the Islamic calendar. In Mauritania, the three-day festival is called Tabaski. It is traditional to kill a ram, and the meat is later cooked and eaten. Khadija and her sister watch the ram being washed as part of the ceremony. Like other families who can afford it, Khadija's family celebrates by sharing their food with poorer families.

Khadija helps wash all the family's clothes before Tabaski. For the festival, everyone wears new clothes that they have bought or received as gifts. Khadija changes her clothes as often as her mother will let her.

As part of the dressing up for the festival, Khadija has her hands and feet decorated with patterns painted with henna, a vegetable dye. She has her hair washed and goes to the hairdresser to have it specially styled.

"I don't like having my hair washed. The soap gets in my eyes, and the comb pulls my hair until it hurts."

Khadija enjoys a special holiday meal called *thieboudjen*. A whole fish is served with spicy rice and vegetables—carrots, radish, yellow peppers, and cabbage. Afterwards, she has a drink made of boiled rice and milk called *gossi*.

"My favorite drink is tufam. It is sour milk and sugar. We drink it when the weather is hot, because it makes you feel fresh when you are tired."

Khadija and her friends go from house to house asking friends and relatives for gifts. Visitors who come to their house also give them small gifts and money.

"I will spend all my money on cake and soft drinks. At the market they pour our drinks into plastic bags."

U.S.A.

Dahlys Ang lives in a town called Arcadia, near Los Angeles, California. Her home is not far from the Pacific Ocean, but the climate is very dry, because of the mountains to the north and the Mojave Desert to the east. It hardly ever rains, so extra water has to be pumped in from the Colorado River.

Dahlys lives with her parents and two younger sisters. Her father works as an accountant and her mother stays at home. Her family eats dinner together every night; the children take turns saying grace. There is always a big jug of water on the table. Each girl drinks from her own glass. Dahlys has a yellow one.

Even though she can turn on a tap to get as much hot and cold running water as she wants, Dahlys has learned at school that water is precious, especially in places where there is little rain. She takes care not to leave the tap running when she washes her hands and brushes her teeth.

"I only use water to clean my toothbrush or to rinse the soap off my hands. I remind my parents and sisters to turn off the tap, too."

Dahlys's family also buys water in bottles. She takes a small bottle to school or when she plays a sport. Big bottles are used for drinking and cooking. They also store bottled water in case of an emergency, such as an earthquake, when the water supply might be cut off.

At eight years old, Dahlys is able to help around the house. She loads dirty clothes into the washing machine and stacks the dishwasher with dirty dishes.

Dahlys is in charge of the family pets—two cats and two goldfish. Every day, she feeds the cats and gives them fresh water to drink. She is teaching her sisters how to feed the fish and change the water in their tanks.

"I like watering the plants and feeding the fish. I don't like doing the laundry or rinsing the dishes."

When she is on vacation from school, Dahlys likes to spend time gardening at home. Her mother has made a small vegetable patch in their garden, so Dahlys and her sisters are learning how to grow food. So far, they have grown squashes, cucumbers, and tomatoes.

Dahlys saves the water that her mother uses for cooking, so that she can use it later to water the plants. After watering the flowers in the garden, she brings all the potted plants from the house out to the patio and gives them a good drink of water, too.

"At school I learned that if we don't save water, we will have less for everyone to drink. Now, I remind Mom to save the cooking water for the plants."

When she goes shopping for groceries with her mother, Dahlys likes to stop to look at the flowers outside the grocery store. They smell so good that she would like to take them all home with her.

Dahlys's mother teaches her how important it is to have clean water. She shows the girls a sign painted on the pavement, on top of the cover for a drain. The sign warns people not to dump anything into the drain, because it carries water into the Pacific Ocean.

The beach is not far from where Dahlys lives, and she loves going there in the summer.

"Every day at sunset we go swimming in the sea, then we play on the sand and collect shells. I like floating in the ocean."

A special day for Dahlys: A hike with Dad

Dahlys and her sisters enjoy helping to wash the family car on the weekend. They use just one bucket of soapy water before they rinse the car with the hose and polish it dry. Then Dahlys and her father drive off in their clean and shiny car to go to the mountains for a hike.

The mountain land is extremely dry and very little grows there. Because this part of southern California is so dry, water is pumped in from northern California and from the Colorado River. There are two big water reservoirs in the mountains, but they don't store much water because there isn't enough rain to fill them up. Dahlys's father tells her that the water level used to be much higher than it is today.

The mountain scenery is beautiful, and Dahlys and her dad have fun walking together. But she is sad to see that some people dump junk here. Dahlys's father explains that trash left around the lakes will pollute the water. Dahlys reads a sign that tells visitors that the water they see here may come out of their taps tomorrow, so they should take care to keep the water clean.

"My wish about water is that people would stop throwing trash in the ocean and keep the water clean for everyone. If you see trash near the lake or on the beach, you should pick it up and take it away so that it doesn't go in the water."

Dahlys is hot and tired after her long hike in the mountains. When she gets home, she is very happy to jump into the swimming pool and enjoy the cool, refreshing water with her father and sisters.

Bangladesh

Mohammed Golam Sadik Saran (or Saran for short) lives in Gaibandha in northern Bangladesh. The village where he lives is surrounded by rivers, so the land is very fertile. Most people are farmers or fishermen. It is hot and rainy in summer, and sometimes the rivers flood. Saran loves to splash in the ponds near his home or take a boat on the river.

Saran is eight years old. He lives with his parents and two older brothers, as well as some of his aunts, uncles, grandparents, and younger cousins. His father owns a pharmacy in the town and he also shares a farm with Saran's uncles. They grow sugarcane, potatoes, onions, eggplant, okra, garlic, and ginger. Saran's house has a big courtyard where grain is laid out to dry after it is harvested.

"We have a machine that goes deep into the ground and pumps water for all the farmland. I help to scatter the seeds for the crops. Sometimes I water the plants and plant the seeds in the ground."

Because it is so hot, Saran likes to wash three times a day—before school, when he gets home in the afternoon, and before he goes to bed. He also washes his own shirt after school. He brushes his teeth three times a day.

"I use four mugs of water for my morning wash, and one mug in the afternoon and evening."

Saran collects water for his bath from one of the three pumps in his home. These are called tube wells and they pump up water from underground. The water is used for bathing, washing clothes, cooking, and drinking. Clothes are washed outdoors, first in the ponds that belong to Saran's family, then a second time in water from the tube wells.

"When you pump the handle of the tube well, water comes out. You collect it in a bucket, mug, or water bottle."

27

After eating some rice for breakfast, Saran gets a ride to school on a rickshaw. The school is in the main town, too far for Saran to walk there from his home.

Saran brings drinking water from home in a plastic bottle. When the bottle is empty, he fills it up from one of the taps and tube wells at school.

Saran keeps cool by splashing his face with water from a tube well in the playground. The playground is sprayed with water to stop the wind blowing dust and sand into the classrooms.

"It is so hot! I drink lots of water, because I feel so thirsty."

When he gets home, Saran has a snack of rice with sugar and milk and a short nap before doing his homework. He also helps on the farm, giving the calves a drink and looking after the pigeons.

"We have cattle, sheep, hens, ducks, and pigeons. They all need lots of water."

The pigeons are Saran's favorites. Sometimes an injured bird falls into the pond, and Saran must jump in to rescue it before it drowns.

Saran finds thunder and lightning scary, especially at night, but he enjoys the rain. He likes to walk around the farm, looking at the animals and birds.

"When there is too much rain, the river bursts its banks and there are floods. There is water everywhere. Houses can be flooded and people can drown."

A special day for Saran: A family trip to the river

Today is Friday, a day of rest. Saran is excited because the whole family is going on a trip to the river. He likes to keep his room clean and tidy, so he makes his bed and sweeps it with a broom made of reeds.

Saran walks with his father and brothers to the nearby mosque. Following the Muslim custom, he washes his face, hands, and feet before prayer.

Later, he enjoys a special meal of chicken with spices, fish, rice, vegetables, and sweet cakes.

After a short nap, Saran is ready to have fun. He is good at drawing and singing, but his favorite game is cricket. Sometimes he and his friends play for hours. They get hot and dusty after a long game, then they run and jump straight into the nearby pond.

"My friends and I splash each other and we play with a ball. Sometimes I go into the ponds and collect water hyacinths with my own hands."

In the evening, everyone dresses up for a sunset boat trip on the river. They visit small islands that sink below the water when the river is full and appear again in the dry season. Saran is happy to be on the water with his family, watching the fishermen casting their nets.

"Water is another name for life. We drink water, we go in boats, and we catch fish. My favorite thing about water is swimming."

Ethiopia

Although Gamachu Boru is only seven years old, he has an important job looking after animals. He lives in a village in southern Ethiopia, where it is very dry. Gamachu belongs to the Borana people who keep cattle, camels, goats, sheep, and sometimes horses. Water and grazing for the animals are the most important parts of their lives.

Gamachu lives with his parents, three sisters, and brother, as well as his sister's two children. The calves sleep inside with the family until they are about two years old, to keep them safe from wild animals. All the children help by taking the family's animals out to find water.

"I don't go to school because I look after the calves. When my brother is old enough to look after them by himself, then I will go to school."

It is difficult to grow food because there is little rain, so Gamachu's family usually buy their maize, a type of corn. Gamachu eats maize porridge when he gets back from his day with the calves.

"I grind the maize every day, then my mother separates the kernel from the husks. She puts a pot of water on the fire and adds the maize to it."

People in the Borana community spend most of their time walking to and from the water holes. In the dry season, the men are sometimes away for days with the animals. The women and girls collect water for the family's washing and cooking. Gamachu's mother walks for three hours twice a day to fetch water from the nearest pond. Donkeys help to carry the heavy water containers.

Early every morning, Gamachu sets off with the calves for the pond. He is out for more than ten hours and doesn't come back until the sun sets. He takes a bottle with a little milk for his lunch. He will add water to the milk when he reaches the pond, to make it last longer and to quench his thirst better.

Gamachu meets up with friends who are also looking after their families' animals. They play games while the calves graze.

"I like playing toki [jacks]. We wrestle, we sing, we swim in the pond, and we make animals from clay. We make camels, cattle, and horses."

A stick from an andarak or an adea plant makes a good toothbrush. Gamachu knows how to find the right plants. He doesn't need water to clean his teeth this way.

"I take a stick with me when I go with the calves, or I find one on the way to the pond."

When he gets to the pond, he washes himself and fills up his bottle with water. The ponds are there only when rainwater fills them. When the ponds dry up, everyone has to walk much farther to get water from the deep wells.

"During the rainy season the ponds fill up, there is plenty of milk to drink, the cattle don't have to go so far to get water, and I don't get tired."

A special day for Gamachu: A walk to the "singing wells"

The pond nearest to Gamachu's home has now dried up, so he must go with his father to take the cattle to the deep wells farther away. Gamachu shares early morning tea with his family before he sets out with his father on the long walk.

The wells are busy in the dry season. When they arrive, Gamachu and his father sit at the top and watch for a while. The animals have to drink in a certain order: horses first, donkeys, then cattle, and camels last of all.

"When there is no water, I wish for water."

A group of people make a human chain to pass the water in buckets from deep down in the well up the steep walls to the top. Those at the top pour it into drinking troughs for the animals. The name "singing wells" comes from the songs people chant as they pass the pails from person to person. This helps them work fast and keep a rhythm as they swing the full buckets up the well and lower the empty ones back down to the bottom to be filled again. The human chain works faster than a machine.

When their cattle have finished drinking, Gamachu guides them away from the well.

"Water is good for everything. The crops grow, it's good for drinking, the grass grows fast, and the cattle don't have to go too far, so they become fat very quickly."

Even after his long walk home from the singing wells, Gamachu still has enough energy to play and dance with his friends.

Tajikistan

Barfimoh Rajabova's first name means snow and moon, because she was born in snowy weather. She lives in Tajikistan, the smallest country in central Asia, which has some of the highest mountains in the world. Barfimoh's village is near the border with Afghanistan.

At eight years old, Barfimoh is the youngest in her family. She lives with her mother and father, some of her ten brothers and sisters, and their children—Barfimoh's nieces and nephews. Like most people in Tajikistan, her family are farmers.

Early in the morning, Barfimoh washes herself and brushes her teeth with warm water. There is no running water in the village, so Barfimoh and her sisters must collect their water from a spring at the bottom of a steep hill. She loves eggs from the family's chickens and eats as many as she can. She even brings some to eat on the journey.

"Chickens need water, or they can't make eggs."

When the weather is warm, the family store all the water they collect in a concrete well. In the cold winter, the water would freeze in the well, so they keep it in pots in the woodshed instead.

"We take our donkey and two big containers. There is a tap and a bucket at the spring. I fill the bucket, then my sister pours it into the containers. It takes about eight buckets to fill them both."

At school, Barfimoh likes to clean the blackboard. The water is kept in a large tin container that hangs on a pole outside the building. The school cleaners bring the water from their homes every day.

"My teacher says we must save water, boil water for drinking, and wash our hands after using the toilet."

When she gets home from school, Barfimoh plays with her favorite lamb. Barfimoh likes to help with the farm animals, which live outdoors behind her house, but she isn't strong enough yet to carry the heavy buckets of water for them to drink.

At home, Barfimoh's sisters do the cooking, the cleaning, and the laundry. They try to use as little water as possible. They heat the water in a wood-fired clay oven.

Barfimoh helps her father in the kitchen garden. The family collects rainwater that runs off the roof of their home. They use it to water their wheat, potatoes, onions, tomatoes, peas, and melons.

"He digs and then I plant the potatoes in their beds. If the potatoes don't get water, they won't grow—they'll stay under the ground."

A special time for Barfimoh: The spring festival of Navruz

Every year on the first day of spring, Barfimoh's village celebrates the ancient festival of Navruz. It means "new day" and marks the return of life after the cold of winter. Everyone dresses in bright clothes for a day of music, dancing, and feasting.

"My favorite seasons are spring and summer."

Navruz is called "the season of the bride." A schoolgirl dresses up as a bride to represent spring. Her attendants carry a platter of sprouted wheat. Sprouted grains are one of the special Navruz foods. They are a symbol of life and health.

Each class in Barfimoh's school prepares a Navruz dish. The children lay out the feast on carpets on the school playing field and the whole village joins in.

Barfimoh enjoys dancing with her friends before she eats freshly baked bread and *dalda*, a soup of fresh herbs, beans, and peas. After the feast, Barfimoh helps to clean out the big cooking pots.

The two-week holiday is a time to plow the fields and sow seeds, spring-clean homes, and cook special dishes using the new crops of spring. Barfimoh's favorite part of the holiday is going into the mountains for the first time in the year to pick herbs.

"Where I live it is very beautiful. If there was no rain, the trees would not be green, the wheat would not grow, the hills would be yellow."

What to Know About Water

Water can contain germs, so many people have to boil it or find other ways to purify it before they can drink it. Tea, coffee, soup, beer, and wine were originally ways to quench thirst without the risks of drinking dirty water.

A tap that drips once a second can waste a gallon of water a day.

Springs and other natural sources of fresh water have to be protected to make sure that the water stays clean.

Water covers about 75 percent of our planet's surface. Between 50 percent and 75 percent of the human body is also made up water.

In richer countries, water is stored in reservoirs before being supplied to people's homes. The first major water storage reservoir in the world was built in 450 B.C.E. in South America and was still in use in the nineteenth century.

The oceans hold 97 percent of the world's water, and 2 percent is frozen in the polar ice caps. That means only 1 percent of the world's water is available for all our needs.

About 2.6 billion people in the world have no access to clean toilets, and 1.8 million children die every year as a result of diseases caused by unclean water and poor sanitation. That's 5,000 deaths a day.

There are 1.1 billion people in the world who don't have access to clean water. That's about one in every six people.

In poorer countries, women and girls can spend up to six hours each day collecting enough water for their families to use. The heavy containers can give them back pain and other health problems.

A person can live for several weeks without food, but only a few days without water.

Glossary

Peru

alpaca – A South American mammal with long, soft hair.

civil engineer – Someone involved with designing, building, or repairing roads, bridges, or tunnels.

climate change – A term used to describe long-term changes in the weather or seasons, meaning that some places are wetter or drier than they used to be, and some parts of the world are hotter or colder.

glacier – A very slow-moving frozen river or mass of ice.

tick – An insect that sucks blood from the skin of warm-blooded animals. Ticks must be removed because they can pass on diseases.

Mauritania

Eid al-Adha – A festival when Muslims remember the story of Ibrahim's (Abraham's) sacrifice.

gossi – A drink made of boiled rice and milk.

henna – A red plant dye that is used to color hair and decorate skin.

ram – A male sheep.

Sahara – A vast desert that covers a large part of northern Africa, from the Atlantic Ocean to the Nile River in Egypt.

Tabaski – The name for Eid al-Adha in some West African countries.

thieboudjen – A fish dish with spicy rice and vegetables, served as part of the Tabaski celebrations.

tufam – A drink made with sour milk and sugar.

U.S.A.

Colorado River – A river that flows through the southwestern U.S.A. into Mexico. It is more than 1,400 miles long.

drains – Underground tunnels that carry water away to rivers or seas.

earthquake – A shaking of the ground caused by volcanic activity or pressure from deep beneath the earth's surface. Earthquakes often damage buildings and disrupt electricity and water supplies.

grace – A prayer of thanks, often spoken before a meal.

Mojave Desert – A desert in southern California and parts of Nevada, Utah, and Arizona.

Pacific Ocean – The largest of the earth's oceans, stretching from Asia and Australia to North America and South America.

pollute – To make air, land, or water dirty or unhealthy.

reservoir – An artificial lake used to collect and store water to supply a town or city.

squash – A vegetable in the gourd family; pumpkin is a type of squash.

Bangladesh

crops – Plants that produce food, such as rice or wheat, or other useful produce, such as cotton.

eggplant – A dark purple fruit that is eaten as a vegetable.

fertile – A word describing land or soil where plants grow easily.

flood – When river, sea, or lake banks burst, causing water to flow into buildings and across roads. Dirty water that gets into freshwater supplies can cause disease.

ginger – A plant with a spicy root used for cooking and for medicine.

mosque – The Muslim place of worship.

Muslim – A follower of Islam.

okra – A thin green vegetable.

rickshaw – A kind of tricycle that carries one or two passengers.

sugarcane – The plant from which refined sugar is made.

tube well – A pump that brings water from wells deep underground.

water hyacinth – A plant with flowers that float on the water, like a water lily.

Ethiopia

graze – How cattle, horses, sheep, or other plant-eating animals feed.

husks – The outer covering of some plants.

kernel – The center of a nut or the stone of a fruit, also the seed of a cereal or grain.

maize – A type of corn.

singing wells – Deep wells where people chant songs as they pass water up the steep sides in buckets.

toki – A game like jacks.

water hole – A natural pond or pool used by people and animals.

Tajikistan

dalda – A soup made of herbs.

Navruz – A festival that celebrates the arrival of spring.

platter – A large, shallow plate used for serving food.

spring – A source of freshwater that naturally flows from underground.

About
the Countries

Peru

✧ About 70 percent of Peru's population lives along the coast, where less than 2 percent of the country's water resources are found.

✧ Lake Titicaca, the largest lake in South America, is on the border between Peru and Bolivia.

Mauritania

✧ The Senegal River forms the border between Mauritania and Senegal.

✧ Most of the fresh water in Mauritania is used for agriculture.

✧ The country's annual rainfall is only about an inch per year.

U.S.A.

✧ The five bodies of water that comprise the Great Lakes (Lake Superior, Lake Huron, Lake Ontario, Lake Erie, and Lake Michigan) form the largest chain of freshwater lakes on Earth.

✧ About half the coastline of the United States is in Alaska.

Bangladesh

✧ Three large rivers run through Bangladesh: the Ganges, the Brahmaputra, and the Meghna.

✧ Because the country is low-lying, about 22 percent of it is flooded each year.

Ethiopia

✧ Ethiopia is a landlocked country—it is surrounded by land on all sides.

✧ Although there are several lakes in the Ethiopian Rift Valley, many of them are alkaline. An alkaline lake is a kind of salt lake.

Tajikistan

✧ There are approximately 1,300 natural lakes in Tajikistan.

✧ Most of Tajikistan's water resources are from melting glaciers and precipitation.